GW01403172

# Integrated Work Life Synergy

chaminda malalasekara

Published by chaminda malalasekara, 2024.

INTEGRATED WORK LIFE SYNERGY

**First edition. October 8, 2024.**

Copyright © 2024 chaminda malalasekara.

ISBN: 979-8227734662

Written by chaminda malalasekara.

## Acknowledgment

I would like to express my heartfelt gratitude to the late Dr. Ranjan Madanayake, my Ph.D. supervisor, whose guidance and support were instrumental in the completion of my research. His unwavering dedication to academic excellence and profound insights have left a lasting impact on my work and personal development.

I extend my sincere appreciation to the academic staff of Texila American University and the Central University of Nicaragua. Their encouragement, expertise, and constructive feedback throughout my academic journey have been invaluable. The collaborative environment and resources provided by these institutions greatly contributed to my growth as a scholar.

I am deeply grateful to my family members for their unwavering support and encouragement. A special mention goes to C.N. Randeer, my good friend and sister, whose assistance in refining the language of this thesis was invaluable. Her meticulous attention to detail and command of the English language greatly enhanced the quality of my work.

This thesis would not have been possible without the support and encouragement of all the mentors, colleagues, and loved ones I had the privilege to work with during my studies.

# Table of Contents

## Introduction:
## Integrated Work-Life Synergy (IWLS) Theory

The Integrated Work-Life Synergy (IWLS) Theory, introduced by Dr. Chaminda Malalasekara in his Ph.D. thesis, represents a significant advancement in understanding and enhancing employee performance through the lens of work-life balance. Unlike traditional models that often treat work and personal life as separate domains, the IWLS Theory emphasizes the interconnectedness and mutual influence between these aspects of an individual's life.

### Core Principles of IWLS Theory:

1. **Synergy between Work and Life:** IWLS Theory posits that work and personal life are not mutually exclusive but rather synergistic. By integrating and aligning personal values, goals, and aspirations with professional responsibilities, employees can achieve a more harmonious balance that fosters increased satisfaction and productivity.

2. **Dynamic Interaction:** The theory highlights the dynamic interaction between work and life domains. It suggests that positive experiences and achievements in one area can spill over and enhance performance in the other. For instance, personal well-being and fulfillment can lead to improved focus and effectiveness at work.

3. **Holistic Approach:** IWLS Theory advocates for a holistic approach to employee well-being. It encourages organizations to consider various facets of employees' lives, including emotional, social, and psychological aspects, and to implement strategies that support their overall quality of life.

4. **Customized Solutions:** Recognizing that work-life balance is not a one-size-fits-all concept, the IWLS Theory promotes customized solutions tailored to individual needs and organizational contexts. This personalization helps address

unique challenges and leverage specific opportunities for each employee.

5. **Enhanced Performance and Satisfaction:** By fostering an environment where employees can seamlessly integrate their work and personal lives, the IWLS Theory aims to boost job satisfaction, reduce stress, and ultimately enhance overall workplace performance.

Dr. Malalasekara's IWLS Theory provides a fresh perspective on achieving work-life balance, offering practical insights and strategies for organizations seeking to improve employee engagement, well-being, and productivity. It underscores the importance of viewing work and life as interconnected elements that, when managed effectively, can lead to greater success and fulfillment in both domains.

**Embracing Integrated Work-Life Synergy**

The boundary between work and personal life has become increasingly difficult to define in today's fast-paced world. The evolution of technology, globalization, and changing social dynamics have blurred the lines between our professional responsibilities and personal commitments. As a result, the traditional concept of work-life balance has proven inadequate in addressing the modern challenges faced by individuals, organizations, and society at large. This book introduces the Integrated Work-Life Synergy (IWLS) Theory, a comprehensive framework designed to redefine how we approach the relationship between work and personal life.

The IWLS Theory is rooted in the idea of synergy—the creation of a whole that is greater than the simple sum of its parts. Unlike conventional work-life balance models, which often view work and personal life as competing forces to be balanced, IWLS focuses on integration, aiming to create a harmonious relationship that enhances both. The core of IWLS lies in understanding that work and life are not opposing domains but interconnected spheres that, when aligned, can mutually benefit and enrich one another. This perspective shifts the focus from merely managing conflict between work and personal responsibilities to actively seeking synergy that drives growth, fulfillment, and overall well-being.

Work-life synergy is not just about achieving happiness outside of work but also about realizing one's full potential within the workplace. IWLS emphasizes the importance of creating a supportive environment that enables employees to thrive in both their professional and personal lives. By fostering this synergy, organizations can unlock the full potential of their workforce, resulting in higher productivity, greater job satisfaction, and a more resilient and effective organization. This book will explore how IWLS can be implemented at both individual and organizational levels, demonstrating the power of a holistic approach to work-life integration.

The IWLS Theory is built upon foundational concepts in psychology, management, and social science, integrating aspects of well-being, productivity, and human connection. Throughout this book, we will explore how these theoretical foundations converge to form a practical framework for individuals and organizations. We will delve into real-world case studies, share the experiences of organizations that have adopted IWLS, and provide practical tools and strategies for successfully implementing IWLS practices in various settings.

Readers will be guided through the journey of transforming their perspective on work and personal life. For individuals, this journey will involve developing strategies to integrate work and personal commitments, enabling a more fulfilling and enriched life. For leaders and organizations, this book offers insights into how to create a work environment that supports integration and synergy, ultimately leading to better employee performance, increased engagement, and organizational success.

In today's competitive and rapidly changing world, organizations must look beyond traditional productivity measures to create sustainable value. The Integrated Work-Life Synergy Theory offers a transformative approach to achieving this by recognizing that when people feel empowered to integrate their personal and professional lives, they are more motivated, innovative, and effective. The benefits of IWLS extend beyond individual well-being; they impact organizational culture, community development, and societal growth.

As you read this book, you will learn about the key principles and components of IWLS, understand the benefits and challenges of implementing this model, and discover best practices for creating a work environment that fosters integration and synergy. Whether you are an individual seeking to improve your work-life experience, a manager interested in enhancing team productivity, or a leader aiming to transform your organizational culture, the concepts of IWLS will provide you with the knowledge and tools needed to create meaningful change.

Together, let us embark on this journey to redefine the relationship between work and life, embracing integration and synergy as the keys to unlocking the full potential of individuals and organizations alike. Through the Integrated Work-Life Synergy Theory, we envision a future where work and life are not opposing forces but partners that, when combined, create a more fulfilling and prosperous existence for all.

This introduction sets the stage for the rest of the book by defining the core ideas of IWLS, outlining its significance, and engaging readers with the promise of practical and transformative insights.

# Chapter 1:

## The Evolution of Work-Life Balance

### 1.1 Introduction: The Changing Landscape of Work and Life

The world of work has changed dramatically over the past few decades. With technological advances, globalization, and the emergence of a digital economy, the way we live and work has become more intertwined than ever before. The traditional nine-to-five work structure, once perceived as the ideal format for separating professional and personal life, has gradually faded. Today, many employees find themselves answering emails at midnight, attending virtual meetings from home, or blending family time with remote work commitments. The boundaries between work and personal life have blurred, and the concept of work-life balance is undergoing a significant transformation.

This chapter delves into the historical evolution of work-life balance, examining the challenges of the traditional balance approach and exploring why a shift towards work-life integration is not only necessary but inevitable. The Integrated Work-Life Synergy (IWLS) Theory emerges from this evolving landscape as a solution designed to enhance the relationship between work and personal life, allowing individuals and organizations to thrive in a more holistic manner.

## Journey to Integrated Work-Life Synergy

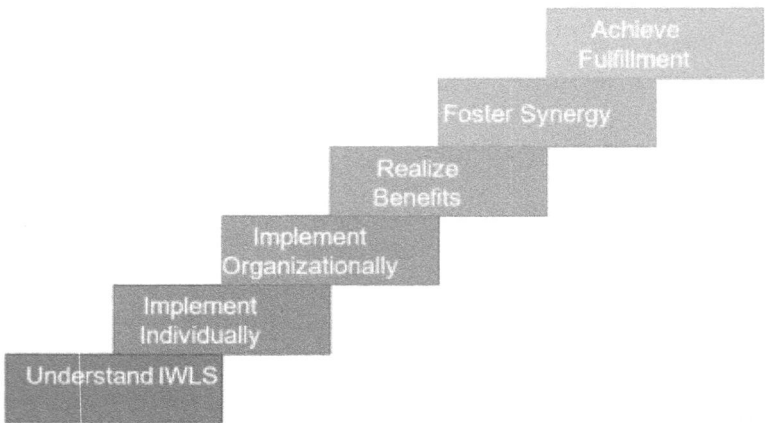

Achieve Fulfillment

Foster Synergy

Realize Benefits

Implement Organizationally

Implement Individually

Understand IWLS

## 1.2 Historical Context: The Traditional Concept of Work-Life Balance

The concept of work-life balance originated during the industrial revolution, as labor unions pushed for better working conditions, shorter hours, and adequate time off. As work moved from farms to factories, and later to corporate offices, the emphasis shifted to creating clear boundaries between professional duties and personal life. The primary goal was to ensure that work did not encroach on the time needed for rest, family, and personal interests. It was a simple idea: work during designated hours and enjoy life outside those hours. The term "work-life balance" first gained popularity in the 1980s, when dual-income households and rising workplace demands made balancing work and family life more challenging.

The traditional concept of work-life balance focused on establishing a clear separation between work and personal time—ensuring that both realms received equal attention. Employees were encouraged to "leave work at work" and avoid letting personal matters interfere with their professional responsibilities. This separation was largely feasible when work was confined to the physical office and digital communication was limited.

### 1.3 The Shift to Work-Life Integration

The rise of technology and the increasing demands of a competitive global economy have made the traditional work-life balance model obsolete for many people. Smartphones, laptops, and constant internet connectivity have made it possible for employees to work anytime, anywhere. While this flexibility has benefits, it has also made it difficult for individuals to "switch off" from work. The idea of balancing work and life as two separate entities no longer fits the reality of most people's experiences.

With the rise of remote work and flexible schedules, the focus has shifted from balance to integration. Work-life integration refers to the blending of personal and professional responsibilities, recognizing that these areas of life are interconnected and often influence each other. The concept is based on the idea that rather than trying to keep work and personal life separate, individuals should find ways to integrate them to create a sense of harmony. This shift in focus has led to the development of new frameworks, such as the Integrated Work-Life Synergy (IWLS) Theory, that aim to create a more comprehensive approach to managing the complexities of modern life.

### 1.4 Limitations of the Traditional Work-Life Balance Model

The traditional work-life balance model often presents work and personal life as competing forces that must be balanced on a scale. This approach assumes that spending more time and energy on one area automatically means sacrificing the other. However, this "zero-sum" view does not capture the reality of how work and personal life are interconnected.

Several limitations of the traditional model include:

1. **Rigidity**: The traditional approach tends to be rigid, focusing on clear boundaries between work and life. This rigidity often results in increased stress when individuals are unable to maintain those boundaries due to unpredictable work demands or personal needs.

2. **Guilt and Pressure**: The concept of balance implies that individuals should always strive to maintain an equilibrium between work and life, which can create feelings of guilt or inadequacy when this balance cannot be achieved. This pressure can lead to burnout and decreased well-being.

3. **Lack of Flexibility**: Traditional work-life balance does not account for the fact that different individuals have different needs at different stages of life. A one-size-fits-all approach fails to recognize that some people may prefer to focus more on work during certain periods and on personal life during others.

Limitations of Traditional Work-Life Balance Model

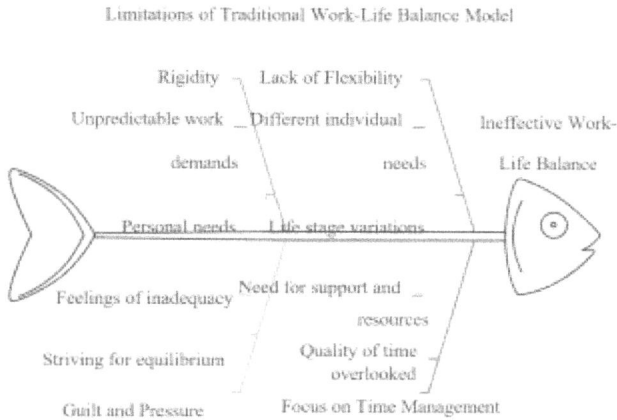

4.

**Focus on Time Management**: The traditional model emphasizes managing time as the primary way to achieve balance. However, it often overlooks other critical factors, such as the quality of time spent, emotional well-being, and the need for support and resources to manage competing demands effectively.

**1.5 The Emergence of Integrated Work-Life Synergy (IWLS) Theory**

Recognizing the limitations of traditional work-life balance, the Integrated Work-Life Synergy (IWLS) Theory proposes a different approach—one that focuses on creating synergy between work and personal life, rather than treating them as opposing forces. The goal of IWLS is not just to manage time effectively but to create a situation where work and personal responsibilities complement and enhance each other.

The IWLS Theory is built on the principle that work and life are not separate domains but are part of an integrated whole. It encourages individuals to find ways in which their professional and personal lives can support one another, leading to greater satisfaction and well-being. By fostering an environment that supports this integration, IWLS aims to help individuals achieve their fullest potential both at work and in their personal lives.

In the next chapters, we will explore the fundamental principles of IWLS, the tools and strategies that can be used to implement it, and the potential benefits for both individuals and organizations. We will also examine real-world examples of how IWLS has transformed workplaces, improving employee engagement, productivity, and overall quality of life.

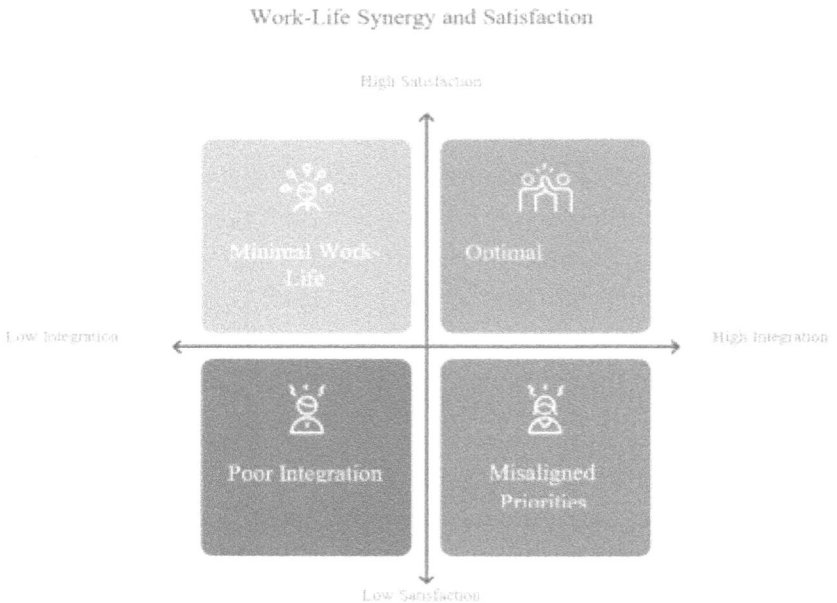

Work-Life Synergy and Satisfaction

High Satisfaction

Minimal Work-Life

Optimal

Low Integration

High Integration

Poor Integration

Misaligned Priorities

Low Satisfaction

## 1.6 Chapter Conclusion: A Call for Change

The changing nature of work demands a new way of thinking about the relationship between work and personal life. The Integrated Work-Life Synergy Theory offers a promising solution to the challenges faced by individuals and organizations today. By moving beyond the outdated concept of work-life balance and embracing integration and synergy, we can create a more sustainable and fulfilling way of living and working.

In this book, we invite readers to explore the IWLS Theory in depth and discover how it can be applied to transform their work-life experience. Whether you are an employee seeking to improve your quality of life, a manager looking to enhance team productivity, or a leader aiming to createa supportive organizational culture, IWLS provides the tools and insights needed to achieve meaningful change. Together, let us embark on this journey towards a more integrated and synergistic future.

This chapter introduces readers to the evolution of work-life balance and provides a foundation for understanding why IWLS is needed. It sets the stage for subsequent chapters that will dive deeper into the principles, implementation, benefits, and challenges of IWLS.

# Chapter 2

## Understanding Integrated Work-Life Synergy (IWLS)

### 2.1 Defining Integrated Work-Life Synergy

The Integrated Work-Life Synergy (IWLS) Theory represents a progressive approach to understanding the relationship between work and personal life. Unlike the traditional concept of work-life balance, which emphasizes a clear separation between work and life, IWLS is based on the idea that work and life are interconnected and can complement each other when managed effectively. The goal of IWLS is to create a state of harmony where both professional and personal spheres contribute to overall well-being, allowing individuals to achieve their fullest potential.

Work-life synergy is about fostering integration that benefits both the individual and the organization. By recognizing the overlap between work and personal life, IWLS encourages the creation of environments where individuals can seamlessly transition between their roles without compromising their well-being. The key to IWLS lies in leveraging the connections between work and personal life in ways that result in mutually reinforcing benefits, creating a sense of synergy that goes beyond balance.

Integrated Work-Life Synergy

Professional Growth

Work-Life Connection

Personal Well- Being

## 2.2 The Pillars of IWLS

The Integrated Work-Life Synergy Theory is built upon four core pillars that support the creation of synergy between work and personal life. These pillars are designed to address the diverse needs of individuals and organizations, ensuring that both can thrive.

### 1. Alignment of Personal and Professional Goals

A core component of IWLS is the alignment of personal and professional goals. This pillar is based on the belief that individuals are most motivated and fulfilled when their work supports their personal aspirations and vice versa. By aligning personal and professional goals, individuals can experience a greater sense of purpose, which leads to enhanced performance and satisfaction.

Organizations can play a critical role in supporting this alignment by helping employees identify opportunities where their work aligns with their personal passions and values. For example, an organization that encourages its employees to pursue meaningful projects that align with their interests can create an environment that fosters greater motivation and creativity.

### 1. Flexibility and Autonomy

Flexibility and autonomy are essential for creating an integrated work-life experience. IWLS emphasizes the importance of allowing individuals to have control over how and when they complete their work, enabling them to manage their personal responsibilities effectively. By providing flexibility, organizations can empower employees to integrate their work and personal commitments in a way that works best for them.

Autonomy is also crucial for fostering a sense of ownership and responsibility. When employees have the freedom to manage their tasks and make decisions about their work, they are more likely to feel invested in their work and take pride in their achievements. Flexibility and autonomy are key factors in creating an environment that supports the integration of work and personal life.

## 1. Supportive Organizational Culture

A supportive organizational culture is vital for the successful implementation of IWLS. Organizations must create an environment where employees feel valued, supported, and understood. This includes fostering open communication, providing access to resources that support well-being, and promoting a culture of respect and empathy.

Managers and leaders play a crucial role in establishing a supportive culture. By showing understanding and empathy towards employees' personal needs and providing opportunities for growth and development, leaders can create an environment where employees feel comfortable integrating their work and personal lives. Supportive leadership is key to building trust and encouraging employees to bring their authentic selves to work.

## 1. Focus on Well-Being

Well-being is at the heart of IWLS. The theory emphasizes the importance of prioritizing both physical and mental well-being as a means of achieving synergy between work and personal life. When individuals feel physically and mentally healthy, they are better equipped to handle the demands of both work and personal responsibilities.

Organizations can support employee well-being by providing access to wellness programs, offering mental health resources, and creating opportunities for relaxation and stress relief. Additionally, promoting a healthy work-life culture that discourages overwork and burnout is essential for maintaining long-term well-being and sustaining synergy between work and life.

## 2.3 The Psychological Foundations of IWLS

The Integrated Work-Life Synergy Theory draws upon several psychological concepts and theories to provide a foundation for understanding how work and personal life can be integrated effectively.

### 1. Spillover Theory

The Spillover Theory posits that experiences in one domain of life (e.g., work) can "spill over" and impact another domain (e.g., personal life), either positively or negatively. IWLS leverages this concept by aiming to create positive spillover effects, where the skills, energy, and satisfaction gained in one area contribute to well-being in the other. For example, achieving success at work can enhance one's self-esteem and positively influence personal relationships.

### 1. Self-Determination Theory (SDT)

Self-Determination Theory emphasizes the importance of autonomy, competence, and relatedness in achieving motivation and well-being. IWLS incorporates these elements by advocating for flexibility, autonomy, and a supportive culture. By providing individuals with the autonomy to manage their work and personal responsibilities, opportunities to develop competence, and a sense of connection with others, IWLS aims to create an environment that supports intrinsic motivation and overall fulfillment.

### 1. Resource-Based Theories

IWLS is also influenced by resource-based theories, which suggest that individuals possess limited resources (e.g., time, energy, attention) that must be allocated across different domains. Effective work-life integration involves managing these resources in a way that maximizes their value across work and personal life. By creating synergy, IWLS seeks to optimize the use of resources, allowing individuals to achieve more with less.

## 2.4 Benefits of IWLS

The benefits of adopting the Integrated Work-Life Synergy approach are manifold, impacting both individuals and organizations in positive ways:

1. **Enhanced Employee Performance**: By creating a work environment that allows individuals to integrate their personal and professional lives, IWLS leads to increased motivation, engagement, and productivity. When employees feel that their personal needs are being met, they are more likely to perform at their best.

2. **Improved Well-Being**: IWLS places a strong emphasis on well-being, ensuring that individuals have the support they need to maintain physical and mental health. By focusing on creating positive spillover effects and reducing stress, IWLS enhances overall well-being and quality of life.

3. **Increased Job Satisfaction**: Employees who experience alignment between their personal and professional goals tend to be more satisfied with their work. IWLS fosters a sense of purpose and fulfillment, contributing to higher job satisfaction and reduced turnover rates.

4. **Greater Organizational Success**: Organizations that adopt IWLS can create a culture of trust, collaboration, and support. This, in turn, leads to greater innovation, reduced absenteeism, and a more resilient and adaptable workforce.

## 2.5 The Role of Leadership in IWLS

Effective leadership is a critical factor in the success of IWLS. Leaders must understand the importance of work-life integration and be willing to create an environment that supports it. This involves leading by example—demonstrating the principles of IWLS in their own lives—and encouraging others to do the same.

Leaders can promote IWLS by:

- **Providing Flexibility**: Allowing employees to have control over their schedules and work arrangements to accommodate personal needs.
- **Offering Support**: Providing resources for well-being, including mental health support and opportunities for personal development.
- **Communicating Openly**: Fostering a culture of open communication, where employees feel comfortable discussing their work and personal challenges without fear of judgment.

## Promoting IWLS

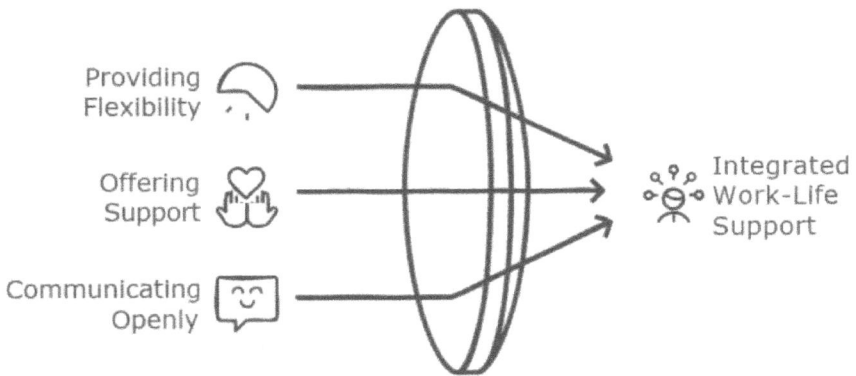

### 2.6 Chapter Conclusion: Moving Beyond Balance to Synergy

The Integrated Work-Life Synergy Theory represents a paradigm shift in how we think about the relationship between work and personal life. By focusing on integration and synergy, IWLS offers a more holistic approach that recognizes the interconnectedness of these domains. It provides a framework for creating environments where individuals can thrive in both their professional and personal lives, leading to greater fulfillment, well-being, and performance.

In the next chapter, we will explore the key strategies for implementing IWLS in both individual and organizational settings. We will look at practical steps that can be taken to foster integration, overcome challenges, and create a culture of synergy that benefits both employees and employers.

This chapter provides an in-depth understanding of the IWLS Theory, its core pillars, psychological foundations, and the role of leadership. It lays the foundation for the subsequent chapters, where practical implementation and strategies will be discussed.

# Chapter 3:

### Strategies for Implementing IWLS in Organizations

### 3.1 Introduction to Implementing IWLS

Implementing the Integrated Work-Life Synergy (IWLS) Theory within an organization requires a strategic approach that takes into account both the needs of the workforce and the organization's objectives. This chapter provides actionable strategies for integrating IWLS into the workplace, fostering an environment where both individuals and the organization can thrive.

Successful implementation of IWLS involves creating policies, cultivating supportive practices, and encouraging a culture that aligns with the principles of synergy between work and personal life. By addressing the practical challenges of integrating work and life, organizations can foster a positive and productive work environment that benefits everyone.

Implementing Integrated Work-Life Synergy (IWLS) in Organizations

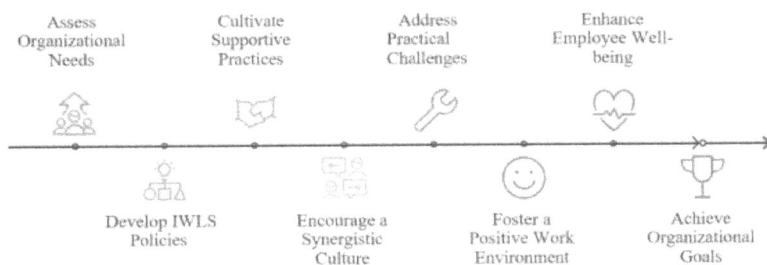

| Assess Organizational Needs | Cultivate Supportive Practices | Address Practical Challenges | Enhance Employee Well-being |
|---|---|---|---|

| Develop IWLS Policies | Encourage a Synergistic Culture | Foster a Positive Work Environment | Achieve Organizational Goals |
|---|---|---|---|

### 3.2 Creating a Culture of Work-Life Synergy

The first step in implementing IWLS is to create a workplace culture that supports the principles of integration and synergy. This involves promoting an environment that acknowledges the interconnectedness of work and personal life, respects employee needs, and encourages them to bring their whole selves to work.

## 1. Leadership Role in Cultivating Culture

Leaders play a vital role in shaping organizational culture. To foster a culture of work-life synergy, leaders should demonstrate empathy and lead by example. This includes being open about their own work-life integration strategies and encouraging employees to prioritize their well-being.

Leaders must also actively communicate the value of IWLS, emphasizing that the organization values and supports employees' personal needs. By being approachable and understanding, leaders can foster trust and create an environment where employees feel comfortable discussing their challenges and seeking support.

## 1. Employee Empowerment and Engagement

Empowering employees is crucial for achieving work-life synergy. Organizations should create opportunities for employees to take ownership of their work schedules and projects. Empowerment involves giving employees the autonomy to make decisions that suit their unique circumstances, which can lead to greater motivation and productivity.

Engagement is another key component of IWLS. Employees should feel that their contributions are valued and that they are an essential part of the organization's mission. By creating a sense of belonging and purpose, organizations can strengthen the link between personal fulfillment and professional performance.

## 1. Addressing Stereotypes and Stigma

One of the challenges in implementing IWLS is addressing stereotypes and stigmas associated with work-life integration. Some employees may fear that seeking flexibility or discussing personal needs will be perceived as a lack of commitment. Organizations need to proactively address these misconceptions by promoting a culture where all employees are encouraged to seek work-life integration without fear of negative consequences.

### 3.3 Policies and Programs for IWLS Implementation

Organizations can create policies and programs that support IWLS. These initiatives should be designed to accommodate the diverse needs of the workforce, providing opportunities for flexibility, growth, and well-being.

### 1. Flexible Work Arrangements

Flexible work arrangements are one of the most effective ways to implement IWLS. By offering options such as flexible hours, remote work, and compressed workweeks, organizations can empower employees to manage their personal and professional responsibilities effectively.

To ensure that flexible work arrangements are successful, organizations should set clear expectations regarding performance and outcomes. Communication is key to making flexible arrangements work, as it allows both employees and managers to align on objectives and avoid misunderstandings.

### 1. Support Programs and Resources

Organizations should provide support programs and resources that address the well-being of employees. This includes access to mental health resources, wellness programs, and family support services. Employee assistance programs (EAPs) can also be valuable for providing counseling and support during challenging times.

Additionally, offering skill-building programs—such as time management and stress reduction workshops—can help employees develop the tools they need to effectively integrate their work and personal lives.

## 1. Professional Development and Growth Opportunities

Supporting employees' personal and professional growth is another important aspect of IWLS. Organizations should offer opportunities for employees to learn and develop new skills, both related to their job and beyond. This can include sponsoring training programs, offering tuition reimbursement, and providing mentorship opportunities.

Professional development is closely linked to personal fulfillment, as employees who feel they are growing and advancing in their careers are more likely to experience satisfaction and motivation. By aligning growth opportunities with personal interests, organizations can create a sense of synergy between work and personal development.

### 3.4 Communication Strategies for IWLS

Effective communication is critical for implementing IWLS successfully. Both leaders and employees must be committed to open and transparent communication to create an environment where work-life synergy can thrive.

## 1. Open Channels for Feedback

Organizations should establish open channels for employees to provide feedback on work-life integration initiatives. This feedback can help organizations understand the challenges employees face and identify areas where improvements can be made. Regular surveys, focus groups, and one-on-one meetings are valuable tools for gathering insights and addressing concerns.

## 1. Promoting Awareness and Understanding

Raising awareness about IWLS and its benefits is essential. Organizations should educate employees on the importance of work-life synergy and how it can positively impact both their personal lives and professional performance. This can be done through workshops, seminars, and informational campaigns.

Employees need to understand that work-life integration is not about compromising on either front but rather finding ways to make both work and personal life more fulfilling. By providing examples of successful work-life integration and showcasing positive outcomes, organizations can motivate employees to adopt IWLS practices.

### 1. Regular Check-Ins

Managers should conduct regular check-ins with their teams to discuss work-life integration and address any challenges employees may be facing. These check-ins provide an opportunity for managers to offer support and make necessary adjustments to work arrangements.

Regular communication ensures that IWLS is not just a one-time initiative but an ongoing practice that evolves based on the needs of employees and the organization.

### 3.5 Overcoming Challenges in IWLS Implementation

While the benefits of IWLS are clear, there are challenges that organizations may face in implementing this approach. Addressing these challenges requires proactive planning and a willingness to adapt.

### 1. Resistance to Change

Change can be difficult, especially for organizations that are accustomed to traditional work structures. Resistance to IWLS may come from both employees and leaders who are hesitant to move away from conventional ways of working.

To overcome resistance, organizations should focus on educating stakeholders about the benefits of IWLS and provide evidence of its positive impact on productivity and well-being. Pilot programs can also be useful for demonstrating the effectiveness of IWLS on a smaller scale before rolling it out across the entire organization.

## 1. Balancing Flexibility and Accountability

One of the concerns with implementing flexible work arrangements is maintaining accountability. Organizations must strike a balance between providing flexibility and ensuring that work is completed effectively.

To address this challenge, organizations should establish clear performance metrics and set expectations for deliverables. Managers should focus on outcomes rather than micromanaging how employees use their time. Regular progress reviews can help ensure that accountability is maintained while still offering the flexibility needed for work-life integration.

## 1. Ensuring Consistent Application

For IWLS to be successful, it must be consistently applied across the organization. Employees should not feel that flexibility and support are available to some but not others. Organizations should establish clear policies that outline the availability of IWLS initiatives and ensure that all employees have equal access.

### 3.6 Measuring the Success of IWLS Implementation

Measuring the success of IWLS implementation is essential to determine its impact and make any necessary adjustments. Organizations should use both quantitative and qualitative metrics to assess the effectiveness of their IWLS initiatives.

## 1. Employee Satisfaction and Engagement Surveys

Employee satisfaction and engagement surveys can provide valuable insights into how employees perceive IWLS initiatives. Questions related to work-life integration, well-being, and overall satisfaction can help organizations understand whether their efforts are having a positive impact.

## 1. Productivity and Performance Metrics

Productivity and performance metrics can also be used to measure the success of IWLS. By comparing productivity levels before and after implementing IWLS, organizations can assess whether work-life synergy has contributed to improved performance. Metrics such as project completion rates, quality of work, and team collaboration are useful indicators.

## 1. Retention and Turnover Rates

Retention and turnover rates are important metrics for assessing the impact of IWLS on employee well-being and satisfaction. A decrease in turnover rates and an increase in employee retention are indicators that work-life synergy initiatives are contributing to a positive work environment.

### 3.7 chapter Conclusion: Laying the Foundation for Success

Implementing the Integrated Work-Life Synergy Theory requires a comprehensive approach that involves cultural change, supportive policies, and effective communication. By creating a workplace environment that values work-life integration, organizations can enhance employee well-being, boost productivity, and achieve long-term success.

In the next chapter, we will explore the role of leadership in greater depth, focusing on how leaders can champion IWLS within their organizations and support their teams in achieving work-life synergy.

# Chapter 4:

The Role of Leadership in Achieving Work-Life Synergy

## 4.1 Introduction to Leadership's Role in IWLS

Leadership plays a pivotal role in the successful implementation of the Integrated Work-Life Synergy (IWLS) Theory. Leaders are not only responsible for setting strategic direction and organizational goals but also for fostering an environment where employees feel empowered to integrate their work and personal lives harmoniously. In this chapter, we explore the importance of leadership in promoting IWLS, the qualities leaders need to cultivate, and specific actions they can take to support work-life synergy.

## 4.2 The Importance of Leadership in Work-Life Synergy

Leaders have a direct influence on the culture and values of an organization. Their actions, words, and attitudes set the tone for what is acceptable and encouraged within the workplace. For IWLS to be successfully integrated into an organization, leaders must:

1. **Act as Role Models** Leaders must embody the principles of work-life synergy themselves. When leaders demonstrate a healthy balance between their professional responsibilities and personal lives, it sends a powerful message to employees. By being open about how they manage their work-life integration, leaders can create a culture of trust and transparency.

2. **Set Clear Expectations and Boundaries** To foster a supportive environment, leaders should establish clear expectations and boundaries regarding work hours, availability, and workload. This can help prevent burnout and ensure that employees feel comfortable managing their time in a way that allows them to focus on both their professional and personal responsibilities.

3. **Encourage Flexibility and Autonomy** Empowering employees to make decisions about their work schedules and how they

accomplish their tasks is key to work-life synergy. Leaders should provide the flexibility employees need to accommodate their unique circumstances, while also encouraging autonomy in decision-making.

### 4.3 Qualities of Effective Leaders for IWLS Implementation

The qualities of a leader directly impact their ability to successfully implement IWLS. Some of the key leadership qualities required for promoting work-life synergy include:

1. **Empathy** Empathetic leaders understand the challenges that employees face in balancing work and personal commitments. By listening actively and showing genuine concern for employees' well-being, empathetic leaders can create an environment where employees feel valued and supported.

2. **Adaptability** Every employee has unique needs, and these needs may change over time. Effective leaders are adaptable and willing to modify policies, work arrangements, and expectations to support employees in achieving work-life synergy. Adaptable leaders recognize that there is no one-size-fits-all approach to integration and are open to experimenting with different solutions.

3. **Effective Communication** Open and effective communication is crucial for promoting work-life synergy. Leaders must clearly communicate their support for IWLS, provide regular updates on initiatives, and encourage feedback from employees. When employees feel that their voices are heard, they are more likely to engage actively in IWLS practices.

4. **Trustworthiness** Trust is a fundamental element of successful IWLS implementation. Leaders must be trustworthy and dependable, ensuring that employees feel comfortable discussing their needs and challenges without fear of repercussions. Building trust helps create a culture of openness

and collaboration.

### 4.4 Leadership Actions to Foster IWLS

To effectively implement IWLS, leaders need to take specific actions that demonstrate their commitment to work-life synergy. The following actions can help foster a supportive environment:

1. **Lead by Example** Leaders should demonstrate work-life integration by modeling healthy behaviors, such as taking breaks, utilizing vacation time, and being mindful of work-related communications outside of regular business hours. When leaders prioritize their own well-being, they set a positive example for employees to do the same.

2. **Promote Flexibility** Offering flexible work options is a key element of IWLS. Leaders should work with employees to identify arrangements that suit their individual needs, such as flexible hours, remote work, or part-time schedules. Leaders should also ensure that policies are applied consistently and fairly across the organization.

3. **Encourage Employee Empowerment** Empowering employees to make decisions about their work fosters a sense of ownership and autonomy. Leaders should provide employees with opportunities to set their own schedules, decide how to complete tasks, and participate in decisions that impact their work-life integration.

4. **Provide Support Resources** Leaders should ensure that employees have access to resources that support their work-life balance, such as mental health services, wellness programs, and opportunities for professional development. By providing these resources, leaders demonstrate their commitment to the well-being of their workforce.

5. **Recognize and Reward Work-Life Integration Efforts** Recognizing and rewarding employees who successfully

integrate their work and personal lives can help reinforce the value of IWLS within the organization. Leaders should celebrate achievements, both big and small, and provide positive reinforcement for employees who prioritize work-life integration.

Foster a Culture of Integrated Work-Life Success

Lead by Example

Promote Flexibility

Encourage Employee Empowerment

Provide Support Resources

Recognize and Reward Efforts

## 4.5 Transformational Leadership and IWLS

Transformational leadership is particularly well-suited for promoting work-life synergy, as it focuses on inspiring and motivating employees to achieve their highest potential. Transformational leaders can play a key role in implementing IWLS by:

1. **Creating a Vision for Work-Life Synergy** Transformational leaders are skilled at articulating a compelling vision for the future. To implement IWLS, leaders should communicate a clear and inspiring vision for what work-life synergy looks like and how it will benefit both employees and the organization.

2. **Inspiring and Motivating Employees** Transformational leaders motivate employees by emphasizing the importance of

their contributions to the organization's success. By showing employees how their well-being is linked to organizational performance, leaders can inspire them to prioritize work-life integration.

3. **Building Strong Relationships** Transformational leaders build strong, trusting relationships with their team members, which is essential for successful IWLS implementation. By fostering a sense of connection and belonging, leaders can create an environment where employees feel comfortable sharing their work-life needs and challenges.

4. **Encouraging Innovation and Creativity** Transformational leaders encourage innovation and creativity, which can lead to new and effective ways of integrating work and personal life. By fostering a culture that values experimentation and continuous improvement, leaders can drive positive change and promote work-life synergy.

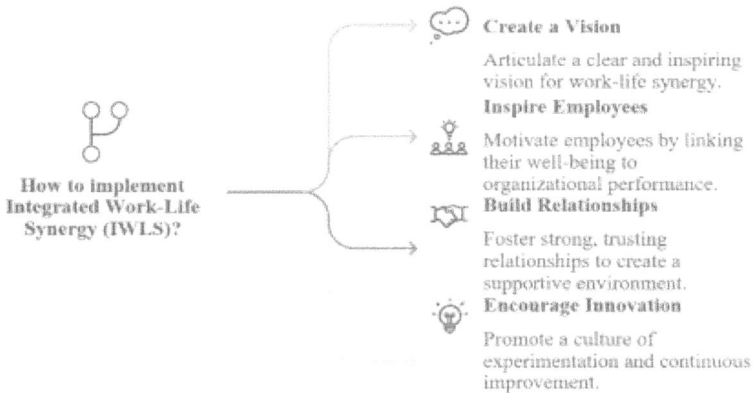

**Create a Vision**

Articulate a clear and inspiring vision for work-life synergy.

**Inspire Employees**

Motivate employees by linking their well-being to organizational performance.

**Build Relationships**

Foster strong, trusting relationships to create a supportive environment.

**Encourage Innovation**

Promote a culture of experimentation and continuous improvement.

**How to implement Integrated Work-Life Synergy (IWLS)?**

## 4.6 Leadership Challenges in Promoting IWLS

While leadership is crucial for implementing IWLS, there are challenges that leaders may face in promoting work-life synergy. Addressing these challenges requires proactive efforts and a willingness to adapt:

1. **Overcoming Resistance to Change** Employees and managers alike may be resistant to changes in work structures, especially if they are accustomed to traditional ways of working. Leaders must be prepared to address resistance by clearly communicating the benefits of IWLS and involving employees in the decision-making process.

2. **Balancing Organizational Needs with Employee Well-Being** Leaders must strike a balance between meeting organizational goals and supporting employees' work-life integration. This can be challenging, especially during periods of high demand or tight deadlines. Leaders should focus on setting realistic expectations and providing the support employees need to manage their workload effectively.

3. **Ensuring Consistency Across Teams** Consistency in applying IWLS principles is essential for fairness and effectiveness. Leaders must ensure that all teams have equal access to work-life integration initiatives and that managers across the organization are aligned in their approach. This may require ongoing training and support for managers to ensure consistency.

## 4.7 Case Studies: Leadership in Action

To illustrate the role of leadership in promoting work-life synergy, this section will provide real-world case studies of organizations where leaders have successfully implemented IWLS. These case studies will highlight the strategies used, the challenges faced, and the outcomes achieved, providing practical examples of how leadership can drive positive change.

1. **Case Study 1: TechCorp** TechCorp is a technology company that implemented IWLS under the guidance of its CEO, who recognized the importance of employee well-being in driving innovation. By promoting flexible work hours, establishing a company-wide wellness program, and leading by example, the CEO was able to create a culture where employees felt supported in balancing their work and personal lives. As a result, TechCorp saw increased employee satisfaction, lower turnover rates, and improved productivity.

2. **Case Study 2: HealthFirst** HealthFirst, a healthcare organization, faced challenges in promoting work-life integration due to the demanding nature of the industry. However, the leadership team took proactive steps to implement IWLS by providing support resources, offering flexible scheduling for healthcare workers, and promoting a culture of empathy and understanding. By prioritizing employee well-being, HealthFirst was able to reduce burnout and improve patient care outcomes.

**4.8 chapter Conclusion: The Power of Leadership in Work-Life Synergy**

Leaders play a critical role in the successful implementation of the Integrated Work-Life Synergy Theory. By embodying the principles of work-life integration, promoting flexibility and autonomy, and fostering a culture of trust and support, leaders can create an environment where employees thrive both personally and professionally.

In the next chapter, we will explore the tools and resources that organizations can use to support the implementation of IWLS, including technology, wellness programs, and professional development opportunities.

# Chapter 5:

**Tools and Resources for Implementing Integrated Work-Life Synergy (IWLS)**

### 5.1 Introduction to IWLS Tools and Resources

Successful implementation of the Integrated Work-Life Synergy (IWLS) Theory requires the use of effective tools and resources that support both employees and the organization. These tools facilitate flexibility, communication, well-being, and productivity, all of which are crucial for achieving synergy between work and personal life. In this chapter, we will explore the different categories of tools and resources available, including technological solutions, wellness programs, support services, and more.

### 5.2 Technological Tools to Support IWLS

Technology plays a significant role in facilitating work-life synergy. By providing tools that enhance communication, collaboration, and time management, organizations can enable employees to work more efficiently while maintaining a healthy balance. The following are some key technological tools that support IWLS:

1. **Communication and Collaboration Platforms** Tools like Slack, Microsoft Teams, Zoom, and Google Meet allow employees to communicate seamlessly and collaborate regardless of location. These platforms enable remote work, facilitate quick discussions, and help employees stay connected with their teams, which contributes to greater flexibility in managing work-life integration.

2. **Task and Project Management Software** Tools like Trello, Asana, and Monday.com help employees manage their tasks, track deadlines, and prioritize work. These platforms enhance productivity and provide visibility into workloads, allowing employees to plan their schedules and maintain a healthy work-

life balance. With clear task assignments and timelines, employees can avoid last-minute pressure and manage their personal commitments effectively.

3. **Time Management and Productivity Apps** Applications like Todoist, RescueTime, and Focus@Will help employees manage their time more efficiently. These tools provide insights into how time is spent, assist with prioritization, and encourage the use of focused work sessions, ultimately allowing employees to accomplish their goals while leaving time for personal activities.

4. **Virtual Workspace Tools** Tools like Notion, Confluence, and Google Workspace provide virtual environments where employees can store information, collaborate on documents, and work together on projects. These platforms create a centralized space for work-related tasks, making it easier for employees to maintain organization while also supporting flexible work schedules.

### 5.3 Wellness Programs to Promote Work-Life Synergy

Wellness programs are a critical resource for supporting employees' physical, mental, and emotional well-being. A comprehensive wellness program can improve employee morale, reduce stress, and enhance overall work-life integration. Below are some key wellness initiatives that support IWLS:

1. **Physical Health Initiatives** Organizations can provide resources that encourage physical activity, such as gym memberships, virtual workout classes, or on-site fitness facilities. Physical health initiatives can help employees maintain energy levels, reduce stress, and improve their overall well-being, contributing to better work-life balance.

2. **Mental Health Support** Mental health is a critical component of work-life synergy. Organizations should provide access to mental health resources, such as Employee Assistance Programs

(EAPs), counseling services, and stress management workshops. Mental health support helps employees cope with personal and work-related challenges, allowing them to maintain a positive outlook and perform at their best.

3. **Mindfulness and Relaxation Programs** Mindfulness programs, such as meditation sessions, relaxation workshops, and yoga classes, can help employees reduce stress and improve focus. These programs promote emotional well-being and enable employees to stay present, enhancing their ability to balance both work and personal commitments.

## 5.4 Employee Support Services

Providing employees with access to support services can enhance work-life synergy by addressing challenges that may arise in both work and personal life. Some key support services include:

1. **Childcare and Family Support** Balancing work and family responsibilities can be challenging for employees with children or dependents. Organizations can support employees by providing access to on-site childcare facilities, subsidizing childcare costs, or offering flexible work schedules to accommodate caregiving responsibilities.

2. **Financial Wellness Programs** Financial stress can significantly impact an employee's ability to maintain work-life balance. Financial wellness programs that provide financial planning resources, workshops on budgeting, and access to financial advisors can help employees manage their financial responsibilities and reduce stress.

3. **Work-Life Coaching** Work-life coaches can provide individualized support to employees as they work towards achieving work-life synergy. Coaches help employees set

realistic goals, develop effective time management strategies, and navigate challenges related to integrating work and personal responsibilities.

### 5.5 Flexible Work Arrangements

Flexibility is a core component of IWLS, and providing flexible work arrangements is essential for promoting work-life synergy. Organizations can offer a range of flexible work options to meet the diverse needs of their employees:

1. **Remote Work Opportunities** Allowing employees to work remotely gives them greater control over their schedules and reduces the time spent commuting. This flexibility can lead to better work-life integration, particularly for employees with caregiving responsibilities or those who prefer working in a comfortable environment.
2. **Flexible Hours** Providing flexible work hours allows employees to adjust their work schedules to fit their personal lives. Employees can start and finish work at times that suit their needs, which can help accommodate family obligations, hobbies, or personal appointments.
3. **Compressed Workweeks** A compressed workweek allows employees to work longer hours over fewer days, such as four 10-hour days instead of five 8-hour days. This arrangement gives employees an extra day off each week, allowing them more time to manage personal responsibilities and rest.
4. **Job Sharing** Job sharing involves two employees sharing the responsibilities of a single full-time role. This arrangement provides greater flexibility for both employees and can help them achieve a better work-life balance by reducing individual workload.

### 5.6 Leveraging Professional Development for IWLS

Professional development opportunities not only enhance employees' skills but also contribute to work-life synergy by fostering a sense of fulfillment and growth. Organizations can support employees in developing professionally while maintaining a balance between their career and personal life:

1. **Online Learning and Certification Programs** Providing access to online learning platforms, such as Coursera, LinkedIn Learning, and Udemy, enables employees to learn new skills at their own pace. Online learning allows for flexibility, making it easier for employees to pursue education without disrupting their work-life integration.

2. **Career Development Workshops** Organizations can conduct workshops and seminars focused on career development, goal setting, and work-life balance. These workshops empower employees to take charge of their career growth while maintaining balance in their lives.

3. **Mentorship Programs** Mentorship programs provide employees with guidance and support from experienced colleagues. Mentors can offer insights into achieving work-life balance, provide career advice, and help mentees navigate professional challenges.

### 5.7 Creating a Supportive Organizational Culture

A supportive organizational culture is essential for the successful implementation of IWLS. This culture should encourage open communication, trust, and respect for employees' work-life needs:

1. **Open Communication Channels** Organizations should create channels for employees to express their work-life needs and concerns. This can include regular check-ins, anonymous

feedback surveys, or dedicated forums for discussing work-life balance.

2. **Recognition and Appreciation** Recognizing and appreciating employees' efforts to achieve work-life synergy is important for promoting a positive culture. Leaders should celebrate employees' successes, both in their work and in their personal achievements, to foster a supportive environment.

3. **Promoting Inclusivity and Diversity** An inclusive and diverse work environment acknowledges that each employee has unique work-life needs. Organizations should strive to create policies and practices that respect and accommodate the diverse backgrounds, experiences, and responsibilities of their workforce.

**5.8 Case Studies: Organizations Using Tools and Resources for IWLS**

To illustrate the effective use of tools and resources for IWLS, this section will provide case studies of organizations that have successfully implemented work-life synergy initiatives:

1. **Case Study 1: CreativeCorp** CreativeCorp, a design firm, implemented IWLS by offering a range of flexible work options, including remote work, flexible hours, and compressed workweeks. In addition to flexible arrangements, CreativeCorp introduced a wellness program that included yoga classes, mindfulness sessions, and mental health support. By leveraging these resources, CreativeCorp was able to increase employee satisfaction, reduce burnout, and boost productivity.

1. **Case Study 2: HealthTech** HealthTech, a healthcare technology company, introduced a mentorship program to

support employees in achieving work-life synergy. Senior leaders provided mentorship on managing work-related challenges while maintaining personal well-being. Additionally, HealthTech offered online learning opportunities for employees to upskill at their own pace. As a result, HealthTech saw improved employee morale, greater engagement, and enhanced retention rates.

**5.9 Chapter Conclusion: Tools and Resources for IWLS**
The successful implementation of Integrated Work-Life Synergy relies on providing employees with the tools and resources needed to support their integration of work and personal life. Technological solutions, wellness programs, support services, and flexible work arrangements all play a critical role in facilitating work-life synergy. In addition, fostering a supportive organizational culture and encouraging professional development are key to ensuring the success of IWLS.

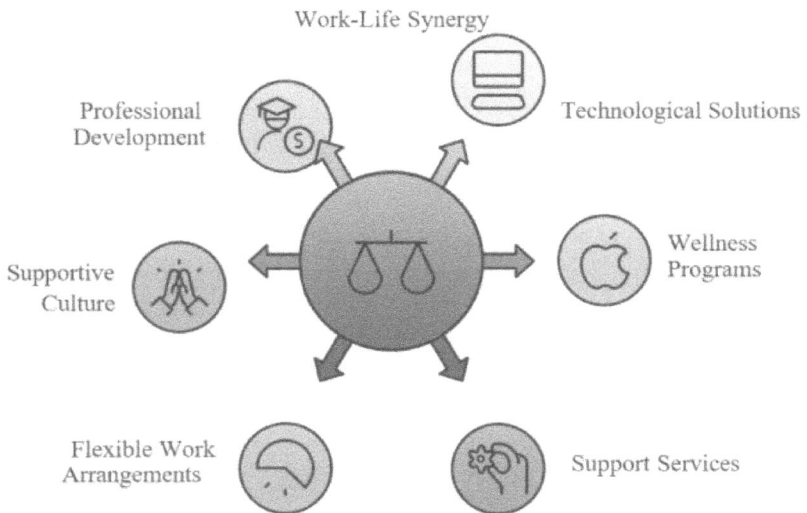

Work-Life Synergy

Professional Development

Technological Solutions

Supportive Culture

Wellness Programs

Flexible Work Arrangements

Support Services

# Chapter 6

The Role of Organizational Culture in Integrated Work-Life Synergy (IWLS)

### 6.1 Introduction to Organizational Culture in IWLS

Organizational culture plays a crucial role in the successful implementation of Integrated Work-Life Synergy (IWLS). Culture shapes the way employees interact, the support they receive, and the norms that guide behavior in the workplace. A supportive culture that values work-life synergy empowers employees to balance their personal and professional responsibilities effectively. In this chapter, we will explore the elements of an organizational culture that support IWLS, the role of leadership, and how to create a culture that promotes work-life integration.

### 6.2 Key Elements of a Supportive Culture for IWLS

A culture that supports IWLS is characterized by several key elements that foster an environment conducive to work-life balance. These elements include:

1. **Trust and Respect** Trust is the foundation of a culture that values work-life synergy. Leaders should trust employees to manage their work while respecting their personal needs and commitments. A culture of trust empowers employees to work with flexibility, knowing that their work-life needs are acknowledged.

2. **Open Communication** A culture that promotes IWLS encourages open communication between employees and management. Employees should feel comfortable discussing their work-life needs, seeking support, and suggesting improvements without fear of repercussions. Open communication helps address work-life conflicts and enables the organization to make adjustments to support employees.

3. **Empathy and Compassion** Leaders who demonstrate empathy and compassion towards employees' work-life challenges create a positive and supportive environment. Understanding the diverse needs of employees and providing individualized support fosters a sense of belonging and helps employees feel valued.

4. **Work-Life Support Policies** Work-life policies, such as flexible hours, remote work options, and parental leave, are an integral part of a supportive culture. Organizations that implement policies aligned with IWLS principles make it easier for employees to achieve work-life synergy.

5. **Employee Empowerment** Empowering employees to make decisions about their work schedules, workload, and career development contributes to work-life integration. When employees have the autonomy to manage their work, they can align their professional responsibilities with their personal goals, leading to greater satisfaction and engagement.

### 6.3 The Role of Leadership in Cultivating Work-Life Synergy

Leadership is a critical component of shaping an organizational culture that supports IWLS. Leaders set the tone for the organization and influence employee behavior and attitudes. Effective leadership for work-life synergy involves:

1. **Leading by Example** Leaders should model work-life synergy by setting boundaries for themselves, practicing self-care, and respecting personal time. When leaders prioritize their own well-being, they encourage employees to do the same, demonstrating that work-life integration is valued.

2. **Providing Clear Expectations** Leaders should communicate clear expectations regarding work goals, deadlines, and performance standards. When employees understand what is expected of them, they can plan their time more effectively,

reducing the likelihood of overworking and work-life conflict.

3. **Offering Support and Guidance** Leaders should actively support employees in their efforts to achieve work-life balance. This may involve providing resources, offering flexible arrangements, or being understanding when personal issues arise. Supportive leaders create an environment where employees feel comfortable seeking help when they need it.

4. **Recognizing and Rewarding Work-Life Balance Efforts** Recognizing employees who effectively manage work-life synergy and rewarding their efforts encourages others to do the same. Leaders can celebrate achievements, both personal and professional, and acknowledge employees' efforts to maintain balance.

**6.4 Strategies for Creating a Culture that Supports IWLS**

Creating a culture that supports IWLS requires deliberate efforts by both leaders and employees. The following strategies can help organizations foster a culture that promotes work-life synergy:

1. **Promoting Flexibility** Organizations should promote flexible work arrangements that cater to the diverse needs of employees. Flexibility allows employees to manage their work and personal commitments, leading to greater work-life integration. This includes options like remote work, flexible hours, and compressed workweeks.

2. **Providing Training on Work-Life Balance** Training sessions on work-life balance, stress management, and time management can equip employees with the skills they need to integrate work and life effectively. Providing training for leaders on how to support employees' work-life needs can also help build a culture that values work-life synergy.

3. **Encouraging Open Dialogue** Creating opportunities for employees to discuss their work-life needs and challenges fosters

a culture of openness. Organizations can establish forums, conduct surveys, or hold one-on-one meetings to gather feedback on work-life integration and identify areas for improvement.

4. **Prioritizing Employee Well-Being** Prioritizing employee well-being should be a core value of the organization's culture. This involves providing wellness programs, promoting mental health support, and encouraging employees to take breaks and time off. A culture that values well-being contributes to employees' overall quality of life and enhances their ability to achieve work-life synergy.

## 6.5 Case Studies: Organizations with Supportive Cultures for IWLS

To illustrate the importance of organizational culture in supporting IWLS, we will look at case studies of companies that have successfully created a culture that promotes work-life synergy:

1. **Case Study 1: Tech Solutions Inc.** Tech Solutions Inc. implemented a company-wide work-life integration policy, which included flexible work arrangements, wellness programs, and regular check-ins with employees. Leadership focused on fostering open communication and trust, leading to increased employee engagement and reduced turnover rates.

2. **Case Study 2: GreenCo** GreenCo, an environmental consulting firm, promoted a culture of work-life synergy by offering flexible schedules, encouraging employees to take time off, and providing resources for mental health support. Leadership led by example by taking breaks and respecting personal boundaries, contributing to a positive work environment that supported employees' overall well-being.

### 6.6 Chapter Conclusion: The Role of Organizational Culture in IWLS

Organizational culture plays a central role in the success of IWLS. A supportive culture that values trust, open communication, empathy, and flexibility enables employees to achieve work-life synergy. Leaders who model work-life balance, support employees' needs, and create an environment that prioritizes well-being are essential for fostering this culture.

# Chapter 7

**Implementing IWLS in Different Industries**

**7.1 Introduction to Industry-Specific Implementation**

The successful implementation of Integrated Work-Life Synergy (IWLS) requires an understanding of the unique challenges and requirements of different industries. Each industry has distinct work environments, employee needs, and operational demands, which influence how IWLS can be effectively implemented. In this chapter, we will explore how IWLS can be tailored to suit different industries, including healthcare, technology, manufacturing, education, and service sectors.

**7.2 Implementing IWLS in the Healthcare Industry**

The healthcare industry is characterized by long hours, shift work, and high-stress environments, making work-life balance a significant challenge. Implementing IWLS in healthcare requires addressing these unique challenges:

1. **Flexible Scheduling for Healthcare Professionals** Shift work is a common feature of the healthcare industry, and offering flexible scheduling options can help healthcare professionals achieve work-life balance. Rotational shifts, shorter shifts, and options for part-time work can provide employees with the flexibility to manage personal responsibilities.

2. **Providing On-Site Support Services** On-site support services, such as childcare facilities, relaxation rooms, and mental health counselors, can help healthcare workers manage their work-life needs. These resources can alleviate stress and provide employees with the support they need to integrate their work and personal lives.

3. **Promoting Mental Health and Wellness Programs** Healthcare professionals are often exposed to high levels of

stress and burnout. Implementing wellness programs, including stress management workshops, mindfulness sessions, and access to mental health support, can enhance employees' well-being and contribute to work-life synergy.

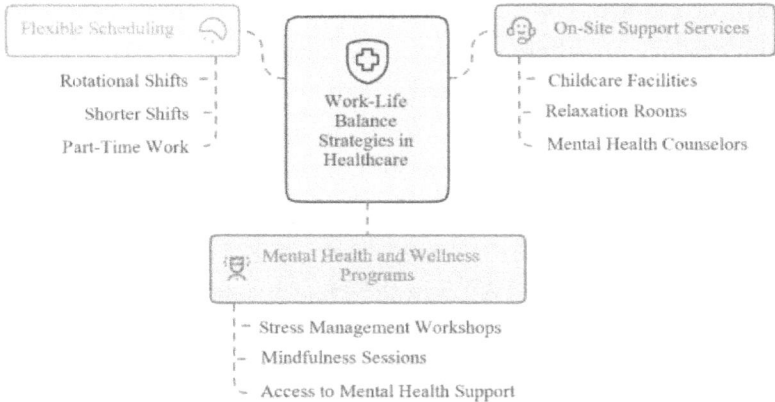

### 7.3 Implementing IWLS in the Technology Sector

The technology sector is known for its fast-paced work environment and the demand for continuous innovation. Implementing IWLS in technology companies involves leveraging flexibility and providing autonomy:

1. **Remote Work Opportunities** Remote work is well-suited for the technology sector, allowing employees to work from anywhere and manage their work-life needs. Providing remote work opportunities enables tech employees to maintain flexibility in their schedules and balance personal commitments effectively.

2. **Autonomy and Empowerment** The technology sector often attracts employees who value autonomy and creative freedom. Implementing IWLS by empowering employees to take ownership of their work and make decisions about their

schedules can enhance their work-life integration and overall job satisfaction.

3. **Encouraging Downtime and Breaks** Encouraging employees to take regular breaks, disconnect from work after hours, and use their vacation time is important in the tech sector, where long hours and high demands can lead to burnout. Leaders should model these behaviors to promote a healthy work-life balance.

Key Components of IWLS in Technology

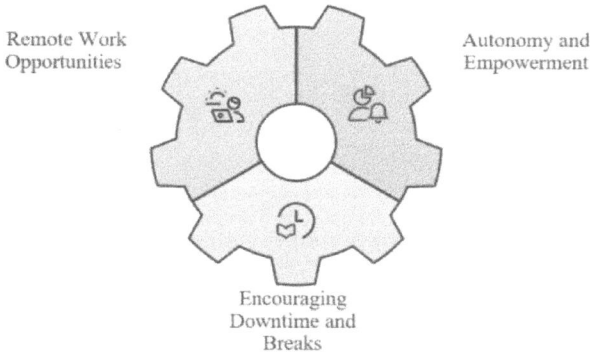

Remote Work
Opportunities

Autonomy and
Empowerment

Encouraging
Downtime and
Breaks

## 7.4 Implementing IWLS in Manufacturing

The manufacturing industry involves hands-on, time-bound work, making flexibility challenging. However, IWLS can still be implemented effectively in this sector:

1. **Shift Swapping and Flexible Hours** Manufacturing employees can benefit from shift-swapping policies that allow them to exchange shifts with colleagues to accommodate personal commitments. Providing flexible hours, where possible, can also help employees manage their work-life needs.

2. **On-Site Wellness Programs** On-site wellness programs, such

as fitness facilities, relaxation areas, and health check-ups, can enhance employees' well-being and support work-life integration. Providing access to wellness resources during breaks can contribute to physical and mental health.

1. **Supporting Families of Manufacturing Workers** Many manufacturing workers have family responsibilities, and providing support for families, such as childcare assistance or family-friendly events, can help employees achieve work-life balance. These initiatives show that

# Chapter 8

**Measuring the Impact of Integrated Work-Life Synergy (IWLS)**

**8.1 Introduction to Measuring IWLS Success**

To evaluate the effectiveness of Integrated Work-Life Synergy (IWLS), organizations must measure its impact on employee well-being, performance, and overall organizational outcomes. Establishing clear metrics and using data-driven approaches can help determine whether the implementation of IWLS is achieving the desired results. In this chapter, we will discuss the various methods and metrics for measuring the impact of IWLS on both employees and organizations.

**8.2 Key Metrics for Evaluating IWLS**

Measuring the success of IWLS requires looking at multiple aspects of employee and organizational performance. The following are key metrics to assess the impact of IWLS:

1. **Employee Satisfaction and Engagement** One of the primary metrics for evaluating IWLS is employee satisfaction. Surveys and feedback mechanisms can help organizations determine if employees feel more satisfied with their work-life balance. High employee engagement is also an indicator of the success of IWLS, as engaged employees are more likely to be productive and committed to their work.

2. **Employee Productivity** Measuring employee productivity can help assess whether IWLS has led to an increase in efficiency and performance. Productivity can be measured through key performance indicators (KPIs), project completion rates, and quality of work. Increased productivity and better-quality outputs are indicators of the positive effects of IWLS.

3. **Absenteeism and Turnover Rates** High absenteeism and turnover rates are often indicators of poor work-life balance. Monitoring these rates before and after IWLS implementation

can help organizations understand the impact of IWLS on employee well-being. A reduction in absenteeism and turnover suggests that IWLS has improved employees' overall work-life balance.

4. **Health and Well-Being Metrics** Employee health and well-being are closely linked to work-life balance. Organizations can use metrics such as stress levels, burnout rates, and the use of wellness resources to evaluate the impact of IWLS. Reduced stress and burnout and increased participation in wellness programs indicate the success of IWLS initiatives.

5. **Employee Feedback and Surveys** Conducting regular surveys to gather employee feedback is a direct way to understand the impact of IWLS on employees. Questions about work-life balance, satisfaction with company policies, and overall well-being can provide valuable insights. Qualitative feedback can also help identify areas for improvement.

## 8.3 Methods for Collecting Data

To measure the impact of IWLS, organizations can use a combination of qualitative and quantitative data collection methods:

1. **Employee Surveys and Questionnaires** Surveys and questionnaires are effective tools for collecting information on employee perceptions of work-life balance and satisfaction. Surveys can be conducted periodically to assess changes in employee attitudes and identify areas for improvement.

2. **Interviews and Focus Groups** Conducting interviews and focus groups with employees provides in-depth insights into their experiences with IWLS. These methods allow for open discussion about challenges, successes, and recommendations for improving work-life synergy.

3. **HR Metrics Analysis** HR metrics, such as turnover rates, absenteeism, and performance appraisals, provide quantitative

data to evaluate the impact of IWLS. Organizations can track these metrics over time to assess changes and determine the success of IWLS initiatives.

## 8.4 Case Studies: Measuring IWLS Impact in Organizations

The following case studies illustrate how organizations have measured the impact of IWLS:

1. **Case Study 1: A Financial Services Firm** A financial services firm implemented IWLS by offering flexible working hours and wellness programs. The organization used employee satisfaction surveys and tracked absenteeism rates to measure impact. Within six months, employee satisfaction increased by 20%, and absenteeism decreased by 15%, demonstrating the effectiveness of IWLS.

2. **Case Study 2: A Manufacturing Company** A manufacturing company introduced shift-swapping policies and on-site wellness programs to support work-life synergy. By analyzing employee productivity metrics and conducting focus groups, the organization found that productivity increased by 10%, and employees reported feeling less stressed and more supported.

## 8.5 Chapter Conclusion: Measuring the Impact of IWLS

Measuring the impact of IWLS is essential for understanding its effectiveness and making necessary adjustments to support employees better. By using a combination of metrics, surveys, and data analysis, organizations can determine whether IWLS initiatives are achieving the desired outcomes, such as improved employee well-being, higher engagement, and increased productivity.

# Chapter 9

Leveraging Technology for Integrated Work-Life Synergy (IWLS)

**9.1 Introduction to Technology in IWLS**

Technology plays a vital role in supporting Integrated Work-Life Synergy (IWLS) by enabling flexible work arrangements, improving communication, and providing tools that help employees balance their work and personal lives. In this chapter, we will explore how technology can be leveraged to implement IWLS effectively and enhance the work-life integration experience for employees.

**9.2 Technology-Driven Solutions for IWLS**

The following technology-driven solutions can support IWLS implementation:

1. **Remote Work Tools** Remote work tools, such as video conferencing software, collaboration platforms, and virtual private networks (VPNs), enable employees to work from anywhere, offering greater flexibility. Tools like Zoom, Microsoft Teams, and Slack facilitate communication and collaboration, making it easier for employees to balance work with personal responsibilities.

2. **Time Management and Productivity Apps** Time management and productivity apps, such as Trello, Asana, and Todoist, help employees organize tasks, set priorities, and manage their schedules. These tools can support employees in managing their workload effectively and achieving work-life balance.

3. **Wellness and Mental Health Platforms** Wellness and mental health platforms, such as Headspace, Calm, and employee assistance programs (EAPs), provide resources to support employees' well-being. These platforms offer meditation, stress management, and mental health support, helping employees

maintain balance and reduce stress.

4. **HR and Employee Self-Service Portals** HR and employee self-service portals enable employees to manage their work-life needs, such as applying for leave, accessing wellness resources, and communicating with HR. These portals provide convenience and autonomy, allowing employees to manage their personal and professional needs efficiently.

### 9.3 The Role of Artificial Intelligence (AI) in IWLS

Artificial intelligence (AI) can play a significant role in supporting IWLS by providing personalized support, automating repetitive tasks, and analyzing employee data to enhance work-life balance:

1. **Personalized Work-Life Recommendations** AI can analyze employee data and provide personalized recommendations for achieving work-life balance. For example, AI-powered wellness platforms can suggest relaxation techniques, exercise routines, or work breaks based on individual stress levels and work patterns.

2. **Chatbots for Employee Support** AI-powered chatbots can provide instant support to employees seeking information on work-life policies, wellness resources, or HR-related queries. Chatbots offer a convenient way for employees to access information and support when they need it.

3. **Predictive Analytics for Employee Well-Being** Predictive analytics can help organizations identify employees at risk of burnout or stress by analyzing data such as work hours, productivity, and absenteeism. By identifying potential issues early, organizations can provide targeted support and interventions to help employees achieve work-life synergy.

### 9.4 Challenges of Using Technology for IWLS

While technology offers numerous benefits for IWLS, there are challenges to consider:

1. **Digital Overload and Burnout** The constant use of technology can lead to digital overload and burnout. Organizations must encourage employees to disconnect after work hours and set boundaries for technology use to avoid negative impacts on work-life balance.
2. **Privacy Concerns** The use of AI and data analytics to monitor employee well-being may raise privacy concerns. Organizations must ensure that employee data is used responsibly, with transparency and consent, to maintain trust and protect privacy.

1. **Ensuring Accessibility** Not all employees may have access to the necessary technology or internet connectivity to participate in remote work or use digital platforms. Organizations must ensure that technology solutions are accessible to all employees, regardless of their circumstances.

## 9.5 Case Studies: Technology-Enabled IWLS Initiatives

The following case studies demonstrate how organizations have leveraged technology to support IWLS:

1. **Case Study 1: A Tech Startup** A tech startup implemented IWLS by using remote work tools and productivity apps to offer flexible work arrangements. Employees were encouraged to use wellness platforms for stress management, and AI-powered chatbots provided instant support. The result was increased employee satisfaction and a positive work-life integration experience.
2. **Case Study 2: A Global Consulting Firm** A global consulting firm used predictive analytics to identify employees at risk of

burnout and provided targeted interventions, such as reduced workloads and mental health support. The use of technology helped the firm enhance employee well-being and reduce turnover rates.

**9.6 Chapter Conclusion: Leveraging Technology for IWLS**

Technology can be a powerful enabler of IWLS, providing tools and platforms that support flexible work arrangements, well-being, and employee engagement. However, organizations must address challenges such as digital overload, privacy concerns, and accessibility to ensure that technology is used effectively.

## Chapter 10
## The Future of Integrated Work-Life Synergy (IWLS)
### 10.1 Introduction to the Future of IWLS

The concept of Integrated Work-Life Synergy (IWLS) will continue to evolve as workplaces adapt to changing employee needs, technological advancements, and societal expectations. In this final chapter, we will explore the future trends in IWLS, the evolving role of organizations, and how leaders can continue to innovate and improve work-life synergy practices to create a sustainable and supportive work environment.

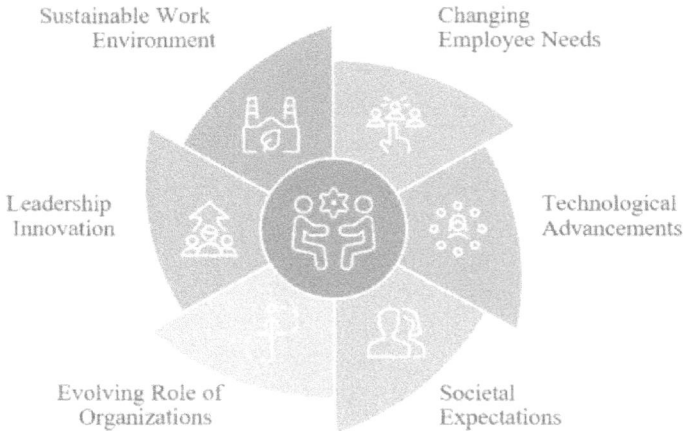

### 10.2 Emerging Trends in IWLS

The future of IWLS will be shaped by several emerging trends:

1. **Hybrid Work Models** The hybrid work model, combining remote and in-office work, will become increasingly common. This model offers employees the flexibility to choose where they work based on their preferences and needs, supporting work-life integration. Organizations will need to develop policies and infrastructure to accommodate hybrid work effectively.

2. **Focus on Employee Well-Being and Mental Health** The importance of employee well-being and mental health will continue to grow, with organizations investing in mental health support, wellness programs, and resources to help employees maintain balance. Work-life synergy initiatives will increasingly prioritize mental health as a critical component of employee well-being.

3. **Personalization of Work-Life Policies** One-size-fits-all work-life policies are becoming obsolete. The future of IWLS will focus on personalization, with organizations offering flexible work arrangements, benefits, and support tailored to individual employee needs. Technology will play a key role in delivering personalized work-life solutions.

4. **AI and Automation for Work-Life Integration** AI and automation will play an increasingly important role in supporting IWLS by automating repetitive tasks, analyzing employee data, and providing personalized support. AI will help employees manage their work more efficiently and create opportunities for better work-life balance.

5. **Emphasis on Sustainable Work Practices** Organizations are recognizing the importance of sustainable work practices that promote long-term employee well-being. The future of IWLS will involve creating work environments that are not only productive but also sustainable, with an emphasis on reducing stress, preventing burnout, and supporting employee health.

### 10.3 The Role of Leaders in the Future of IWLS

Leaders will play a crucial role in shaping the future of IWLS. The following leadership practices will be essential:

1. **Leading by Example** Leaders must model work-life balance by setting boundaries, prioritizing well-being, and demonstrating the importance of taking time off. By leading by example, leaders can create a culture that values work-life synergy.
2. **Fostering an Inclusive Culture** Inclusive leadership is essential for creating a work environment that supports work-life synergy for all employees. Leaders must ensure that work-life policies are accessible and relevant to employees from diverse backgrounds, including those with caregiving responsibilities, disabilities, or other unique needs.
3. **Empowering Employees** Leaders must empower employees to take control of their work-life balance by providing the necessary resources, support, and autonomy. This includes offering flexible work options, encouraging open communication, and supporting employees in making choices that promote balance.

### 10.4 Preparing for the Future of IWLS

Organizations can prepare for the future of IWLS by taking the following steps:

1. **Investing in Technology and Infrastructure** Investing in technology and infrastructure that supports remote work, well-being, and employee engagement will be critical. Organizations must ensure that employees have access to the tools and resources they need to achieve work-life synergy.
2. **Continuous Learning and Adaptation** The work-life landscape will continue to evolve, and organizations must be committed to continuous learning and adaptation. This

includes staying informed about emerging trends, soliciting employee feedback, and making necessary adjustments to work-life policies and practices.

3. **Building a Culture of Trust and Support** A culture of trust and support is essential for successful IWLS implementation. Organizations must foster a work environment where employees feel comfortable discussing their work-life needs, and where leaders are committed to supporting those needs.

## 10.5 Conclusion: The Future of IWLS

The future of Integrated Work-Life Synergy (IWLS) will be shaped by changing employee needs, technological advancements, and a growing focus on well-being and sustainability. Organizations that embrace hybrid work models, prioritize personalization, leverage AI, and foster a supportive culture will be well-positioned to create a positive and sustainable work-life synergy experience for their employees.

As we conclude this book, it is clear that IWLS is more than just a policy—it is a philosophy that requires a commitment to understanding and supporting the diverse needs of employees. By adopting an integrated approach to work-life synergy, organizations can create a more balanced, productive, and fulfilling work environment that benefits both employees and the organization as a whole.

Thank you

all your comment share with chaminmal@yahoo.com

# References

1. Adams, J. S. (1963). *Toward an understanding of inequity.* Journal of Abnormal and Social Psychology, 67(5), 422–436. https://doi.org/10.1037/h0040968

2. Allen, T. D., Herst, D. E. L., Bruck, C. S., & Sutton, M. (2000). *Consequences associated with work-to-family conflict: A review and agenda for future research.* Journal of Occupational Health Psychology, 5(2), 278–308. https://doi.org/10.1037/1076-8998.5.2.278

3. Beehr, T. A., & Newman, J. E. (1978). *Job stress, employee health, and organizational effectiveness: A facet analysis, model, and literature review.* Personnel Psychology, 31(4), 665–699. https://doi.org/10.1111/j.1744-6570.1978.tb02113.x

4. Brown, K. W., & Ryan, R. M. (2003). *The benefits of being present: Mindfulness and its role in psychological well-being.* Journal of Personality and Social Psychology, 84(4), 822–848. https://doi.org/10.1037/0022-3514.84.4.822

5. Burke, R. J., & Greenglass, E. R. (2001). *Hospital restructuring, work-family conflict, and psychological well-being among nursing staff.* Stress and Health, 17(1), 33–43. https://doi.org/10.1002/smi.822

6. Carlson, D. S., Kacmar, K. M., & Williams, L. J. (2000). *Construction and initial validation of a multidimensional measure of work-family conflict.* Journal of Vocational Behavior, 56(2), 249–276. https://doi.org/10.1006/jvbe.1999.1713

7. Frone, M. R. (2003). *Work-family conflict: An empirical review of the 1990s.* In J. C. Quick & L. E. Tetrick (Eds.), *Handbook of occupational health psychology* (pp. 239-267). American Psychological Association.

8. Greenhaus, J. H., & Allen, T. D. (2011). *Work-family balance: A review and extension of the literature.* In R. J. Burke & C. L.

Cooper (Eds.), *The SAGE handbook of organizational behavior* (pp. 165-183). SAGE Publications.

9. Kahn, R. L., & Byosiere, P. (1992). *Stress in organizations.* In M. D. Dunnette & L. M. Hough (Eds.), *Handbook of industrial and organizational psychology* (pp. 571-650). Consulting Psychologists Press.

10. Kossek, E. E., & Ozeki, C. (1998). *Work-family conflict, policies, and the job-life satisfaction relationship: A review and meta-analysis.* Journal of Applied Psychology, 83(2), 139–149. https://doi.org/10.1037/0021-9010.83.2.139

11. Maslach, C., & Leiter, M. P. (2016). *Burnout: A guide to identifying burnout and pathways to recovery.* Harvard Business Review Press.

12. McNall, L. A., Nicklin, J. M., & Masuda, A. D. (2010). *Flexible work arrangements and employee performance: A meta-analysis.* Journal of Management, 36(1), 56–93. https://doi.org/10.1177/0149206308322510

13. Michel, J. S., Kotrba, L. M., Mitchelson, J. K., Clark, M. A., & Baltes, B. B. (2011). *Antecedents of work-family conflict: A meta-analytic review.* Journal of Personnel Psychology, 10(2), 70–81. https://doi.org/10.1027/1866-5888/a000031

14. Rothbard, N. P. (2001). *Enriching or depleting? The dynamics of engagement in work and family roles.* Administrative Science Quarterly, 46(1), 655–684. https://doi.org/10.2307/3090160

15. Schaufeli, W. B., & Bakker, A. B. (2004). *Job demands, job resources, and their relationship with burnout and engagement: A multi-sample study.* Journal of Organizational Behavior, 25(3), 293–315. https://doi.org/10.1002/job.248

16. Siegel, J. P., & Korte, R. F. (2020). *The impact of workplace culture on employee performance: A framework for understanding the complexities.* Journal of Business Research, 119, 325-334. https://doi.org/10.1016/j.jbusres.2020.08.030

17. Thomas, L. T., & Ganster, D. C. (1995). *Impact of family-supportive work variables on work-family conflict and strain.* Journal of Applied Psychology, 80(1), 6–15. https://doi.org/10.1037/0021-9010.80.1.6

18. Wayne, J. H., Grzywacz, J. G., & Carlson, D. S. (2004). *Work-family facilitation: A theoretical model and empirical test.* Journal of Vocational Behavior, 64(2), 290–306. https://doi.org/10.1016/j.jvb.2003.08.003

19. Zedeck, S., & Mosier, K. L. (1990). *Work in the family and employing organization.* American Psychologist, 45(2), 240–251. https://doi.org/10.1037/0003-066X.45.2.240

20. Allen, T. D. (2001). *Family-supportive work environments: The role of organizational perceptions.* Journal of Vocational Behavior, 58(3), 434–450. https://doi.org/10.1006/jvbe.2000.1773

21. Bond, J. T., Galinsky, E., & Swanberg, J. (1998). *The 1997 National Study of the Changing Workforce.* Families and Work Institute.

22. Grzywacz, J. G., & Carlson, D. S. (2007). *Conceptualizing work–family balance: A demands and resources approach.* Advances in Developing Human Resources, 9(4), 455–471. https://doi.org/10.1177/1523422307307570

23. Higgins, C. A., Duxbury, L. E., & Lyons, S. T. (2007). *Impact of workload on the work-life balance of professional and managerial employees.* International Journal of Human Resource Management, 18(4), 703–728. https://doi.org/10.1080/09585190701217036

24. Jansen, P. G. W., & van der Velde, M. E. G. (2001). *Job characteristics and the work-family interface: The influence of job demands and job resources on work-family conflict.* Journal of Occupational Health Psychology, 6(4), 329–341. https://doi.org/10.1037/1076-8998.6.4.329

25. Kahn, R. L., Wolfe, D. M., Quinn, R. P., Snoek, J. D., & Rosenthal, R. A. (1964). *Organizational stress: Studies in role conflict and ambiguity*. Wiley.

26. Kirrane, M. J., & Buckley, F. (2019). *Work-life balance: A review of the literature*. Journal of Management, 45(4), 1320–1345. https://doi.org/10.1177/0149206318758320

27. Kossek, E. E., Pichler, S., Bodner, T., & Hammer, L. B. (2011). *Control at work, control at home: The role of work-family conflict in employee adjustment*. Journal of Organizational Behavior, 32(6), 801–817. https://doi.org/10.1002/job.685

28. Perrewé, P. L., & Ganster, D. C. (2000). *Exploring theoretical mechanisms underlying the effects of stress on health*. In S. L. Sauter, J. J. Hurrell, & C. L. Cooper (Eds.), *History and current issues in job stress* (pp. 95-122). Taylor & Francis.

# About the Author

Biography

I come from a middle-class family in Horowpothana, a rural area in Sri Lanka. With a strong determination to excel academically, I earned a Grade 5 scholarship, which enabled me to attend Kingswood College in Kandy. This pivotal moment marked the beginning of my pursuit of higher education and personal growth.

Driven by a desire to make a meaningful impact, I worked diligently throughout my studies, balancing academic commitments with various work experiences across multiple companies. These experiences provided me with invaluable insights into workplace dynamics and the importance of employee satisfaction and productivity.

My passion for understanding the relationship between workplace happiness and productivity led me to undertake extensive research in this field. My dedication culminated in the attainment of my Ph.D., where I explored innovative concepts and theories to enhance employee well-being and organizational effectiveness.

Through my journey, I exemplify the power of perseverance and hard work, striving to contribute positively to the world of work while inspiring others to find balance and fulfillment in their professional lives.

Milton Keynes UK
Ingram Content Group UK Ltd.
UKHW032322221024
449917UK00001B/60